Rebecca

Becky
Lupp

101 QUICK TIPS
TO MAKE YOUR HOME
SMELL
SenseSational

Books by Terry Willits

101 Quick Tips to Make Your Home
Feel SenseSational

101 Quick Tips to Make Your Home
Look SenseSational

101 Quick Tips to Make Your Home
Smell SenseSational

101 Quick Tips to Make Your Home
Sound SenseSational

101 Quick Tips to Make Your Home
Taste SenseSational

Creating a SenseSational Home

If you are interested in having Terry Willits speak to your
church, organization, or special event, please contact:

InterAct Speaker's Bureau
8012 Brooks Chapel Road, Suite 243
Brentwood, Tennessee 37027
Telephone (800) 370-9932
Fax (615) 370-9939

101 QUICK TIPS
TO MAKE YOUR HOME
SMELL
SenseSational

TERRY WILLITS

ZondervanPublishingHouse
Grand Rapids, Michigan

A Division of HarperCollins*Publishers*

101 Quick Tips to Make Your Home Smell SenseSational
Copyright © 1996 by Terry Willits

Requests for information should be addressed to:

ZondervanPublishingHouse
Grand Rapids, Michigan 49530

Library of Congress Cataloging-in-Publication Data

Willits, Terry, 1959–
     101 quick tips to make your home smell SenseSational / Terry Willits.
        p. cm.
     ISBN: 0-310-20225-6
     1. Dwellings. 2. Odors. 3. Essences and essential oils. 4. Christian life.
  I. Title.
TX303.W55   1996
645—dc20   96-13344
                                               CIP

This edition printed on acid-free paper and meets the American National Standards Institute Z39.48 standard.

Edited by Rachel Boers
Interior Illustrations by Edsel Arnold
Interior design by Sherri Hoffman

Printed in the United States of America

96 97 98 99 00 01 02 /❖ QF/ 10 9 8 7 6 5 4 3 2 1

And the house was filled with the

fragrance of the perfume.

John 12:3

Introduction

— ❧ —

One of God's sweetest gifts to us is the sense of smell. Similarly, one of the most satisfying things we can share with those who enter our homes is pleasant fragrance. Fragrance is a gift that will gratify today and linger in memories long after the scent is gone.

Whether we notice it or not, fragrance fills our lives. Every breath brings the opportunity to smell something wonderful. Unfortunately, it seems the only scents we stop to smell are those that are especially strong. The well-known saying, "Take time to smell the roses," suggests we should slow our lives down more often to enjoy the goodness of life.

May the following tips inspire you to smell the "roses" already in your life, as well as add some new blossoms to your fragrance bouquet. Keep in mind that the purpose of scents is to enhance your home, not overpower it. A few simple touches in each room are all you need. Have fun fragrancing!

terry.

101 Quick Tips
To Make Your Home
❧ S M E L L ☙
SenseSational

Light up your life.

*L*ight a scented candle when you spend time with God. The fragrant smell will calm your spirits, bringing you pleasure and peace while you focus on him.

2

Welcome with a wreath.

Welcome loved ones to your home with a dried floral wreath or bouquet on your front door. A few drops of essential oil on the dried leaves will refresh its floral scent. For a special occasion, tuck fresh, fragrant flowers in a wreath of greenery.

3

Pour it on!

*F*ill a watering can with sweet-smelling fresh flowers. Place it by your front door for a friendly, fragrant greeting.

4

Banish bugs.

To add scent to your home's exterior and to keep bugs away in warm weather, place highly-scented citronella candles by your entrances. They will welcome guests and ward off uninvited insects.

5

Greet guests with geraniums.

*I*n the spring and summer, a basket or pot filled to the brim with geraniums lends warmth and a pleasant fragrance to a sunny entrance. In the winter, bring them indoors to scent a cheery spot.

6

Smell the roses.

*R*oses are among the most preferred and perfumed flowers. Planting one in your backyard will ensure a bounty of beauty and scent for years. When doing other landscaping around your home, select some shrubs that are aromatic as well as attractive.

Live it up!

To ensure the most fragrance, cut fresh flowers from your garden in the morning, while it is still dewy. Extend the life and fragrance of fresh-cut flowers by adding a little chlorine bleach and sugar to luke-warm water. Trim the flower stems and change the water daily.

8

Bring joy with jasmine.

Satisfy a sunny spot of your home with the sweet smell of jasmine. Hang a basket beneath a skylight, sit a pot on a windowsill, or embrace your mailbox with its vines and fragrant blossoms.

Wrap your windows with wonderful fragrance.

*B*uy a beautiful window box and fill it with cascading fragrant flowers and greenery. Consult your local garden center for suitable flowers and plants.

10

Clear the air!

$\mathcal{O}$n a pretty day, open your windows and give your home a good, old-fashioned airing out. Let the fresh breeze sweep through your rooms. Take area rugs outside and shake them well to remove dirt, dust, and musty smells.

11

Filter it.

*C*hange your air filter frequently to clean your home of unhealthy, allergy-aggravating particles that your eyes can't see, but your nose can smell. Attach a Filter Mate to your air filter to scent your home.

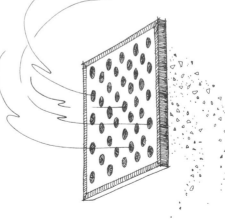

12

Think green.

$\mathscr{F}$ill your home with live plants. House-
plants can enrich your home life, not only by
pleasing your eye, but by cleaning the air
of impurities — they're God's free air
filter system!

13

Turn on the fragrance!

For a safe and easy scent, place a lamp ring on a lamp's light bulb. Add a few drops of essential oil, then turn on the lamp to enjoy the fragrance for hours. To be welcomed with a pleasant-smelling greeting, set the lamp on a timer.

14

Treasure pearls of potpourri.

*T*hese tiny, perfumed pellets can be used in many ways. Place potpourri pearls in lamp rings, potpourri mixtures, dried flowers, simmering water, or a simple bowl to fragrance any room of your home.

15

Welcome warmly.

*L*et the sparkle and smell of a scented candle give a warm welcome that says "home." Place one in your front entrance and powder room to greet guests. Light one by your back door before loved ones arrive home, to let them know you are expecting them.

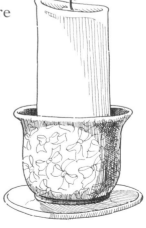

16

Share a sweet aroma.

*K*eep a small bottle of perfume in a basket
near the entrance where you greet family.
A quick spray will make you feel fresh and
will welcome those you love with a sweet
aroma well worth coming
home to.

Enjoy your pets.

Bathe dogs and change cat litter frequently. Your pets and all others who enter your home will appreciate your effort to keep things smelling pleasant.

18

Keep closets fresh as a forest.

$\mathcal{U}$se cedar wood hangers to hang outerwear in your coat closet. They will repel moths and mildew while pleasantly scenting your garments. For an extra, unexpected whiff of fragrance, hide a cedar block or pleasing sachet on the top shelf of the closet.

19

Fire up!

The smell of a wood-burning fire gives the instant impression of warmth and security. Prepare a fire in advance so you can enjoy its woodsy fragrance at the strike of a match.

20

Perfume with pinecones.

*P*ile a basket full of evergreen, cinnamon, or spice-scented pinecones by your fireplace. Toss one occasionally into the roaring flames for a burst of satisfying scent. To fragrance pine cones, simply dot them with a few drops of essential oil.

21

Scent with heavenly herbs.

*H*ighly fragrant herbs can enhance a fire. To scent the room, tie tiny bundles of rosemary or lavender with twine, pile them in a basket, and every now and then toss a bundle alongside flaming logs.

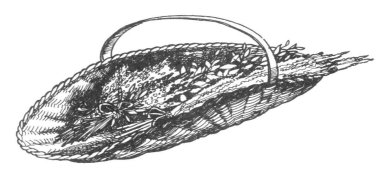

22

Provide pleasure
with potpourri.

 he natural beauty and fragrance of potpourri can enhance any room. Select an appealing, fragrant mixture and display it in a pretty bowl or dish. Revitalize potpourri with an essential oil. Store unused potpourri in an airtight glass jar in your pantry.

Fan the flames.

Place a wooden bowl of pretty, pleasant-smelling potpourri by the fire so that the heat of the flames will warm the mixture and release its scent throughout the room. A handful of potpourri thrown in the fire will also delight your sense of smell.

24

Celebrate the season with scent.

*E*nhance potpourri with a seasonal touch. For a Christmas scent, add a few sprigs of holly, bright bunches of red berries, and cinnamon pinecones. For a fresh, spring fragrance, liven potpourri with lemon peels and dried yellow roses.

Begin a "love bowl."

*B*it by bit, blossom by blossom, build a "love bowl" of potpourri. Pluck petals, leaves, and buds from bouquet stems as you discard them. Dry them and toss them in a bowl with a few drops of fragrant oil.

26

Save it with silica gel.

*D*ry flowers and preserve their vibrant colors by microwaving them with silica gel. Simply spoon silica gel to cover flowers and microwave them a minute at a time, testing the flowers' texture until crisp. Use your dried flowers for potpourri, adding a few drops of essential oil for fragrance.

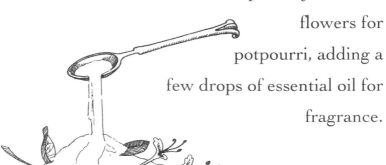

Liven up with lovely scents.

*O*verflow a large vase in your living room with the vibrant aromas of lilac or lily of the valley. These flowers are especially fragrant and will delight all who gather together in your home.

28

Savor the wonderful scent of white.

White flowers are often the most fragrant. Fill a crystal vase with a dozen white carnations or roses and savor their scent and sophisticated simplicity.

Lemon up!

*D*ust wood furniture with a quality, pleasant-smelling furniture polish. For a fresh, lively scent, try lemon. Enhance the fragrance by stashing lemon-scented sachets behind a bookshelf or sofa pillow, or one to a doorknob or arm of a wooden chair.

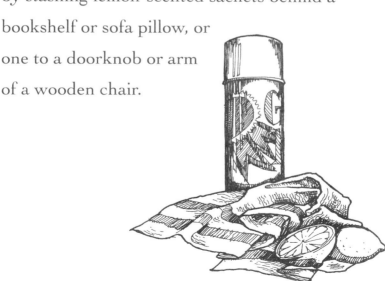

30

Make a sachet
in seconds.

*T*ake a pretty handkerchief or square of
decorative fabric or muslin, spoon in a fragrant
potpourri mixture, and tie it with whatever
seems appropriate — a tassel, ribbon,
raffia, or twine.

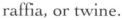

Lemon up!

*D*ust wood furniture with a quality, pleasant-smelling furniture polish. For a fresh, lively scent, try lemon. Enhance the fragrance by stashing lemon-scented sachets behind a bookshelf or sofa pillow, or one to a doorknob or arm of a wooden chair.

30

Make a sachet
in seconds.

*T*ake a pretty handkerchief or square of
decorative fabric or muslin, spoon in a fragrant
potpourri mixture, and tie it with whatever
seems appropriate — a tassel, ribbon,
raffia, or twine.

31

Rub it in.

*R*ub essential oil into the inside of a wood drawer, onto the back of a wood picture frame, or under a wood table. The unfinished wood will slowly absorb and release the oil's pleasant scent. Do not use essential oils on finished wood.

32

Make paperwork a pleasure.

*P*erfume your desk drawers with sachets or enhance your desktop with a single blossoming flower. Light a scented candle to inspire you while you work.

Send a scent.

*A*dd fragrance to your stationary by spray-
ing cologne inside the lid or placing a sachet
envelope in your stationary box. For a special
scented gift, slip a sachet envelope or fragrant
envelope of bath crystals into a
card and mail it to a friend.

34

Share a cup and saucer of scent.

*D*rop a scented votive candle in a pretty demitasse or teacup. Place it on a saucer in a spot looking for a touch of fragrant charm.

Make it a clean sweep.

To eliminate lingering smoky fumes, have a professional chimney sweep perform a safety inspection and clean your fireplace at least once a year.

36

Attract swarms of noses.

*L*ight a long-lasting beeswax candle. Its honeycomb texture and sweet honey scent make it most pleasing.

Bake a batch.

*M*ake a big batch of cookie dough, roll it, and freeze it in wax paper. You can also use ready-made "slice and bake" cookie dough. Whenever the urge hits, bake a batch to fill your kitchen and your stomach with delight.

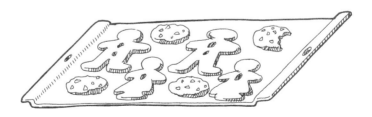

38

Go for the garlic!

*F*or a quick, delicious scent, sauté minced garlic and olive oil in a pan and let it simmer slowly. Whether you toast it on bread or toss it in food to stir fry, the great garlic scent is sure to satisfy.

Cook a turkey, chicken, ham, or roast.

*T*he succulent smell of meat roasting is guaranteed to make your home smell cozy and your mouth water!

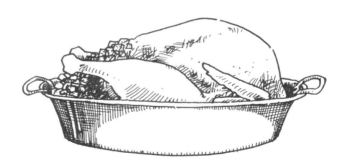

40

Pull out the crock-pot.

There's nothing like coming home to the smell of supper cooking — especially when you're the cook! Use your crock-pot to prepare simple, delicious-smelling dinners.

41

Wake up and smell the coffee!

*L*et the aroma of coffee brewing lure you out of bed in the morning. Make coffee the night before and set a timer to turn it on before your alarm sounds. For a special treat any time, grind fresh coffee beans with a dash of cinnamon.

42

Simmer some soup.

Make a big pot of your favorite soup and let it simmer on the stove. Savor the smell as it steams your kitchen and welcomes family home.

Sprinkle a scent.

Sprinkle carpet fragrance directly on carpet or add to vacuum cleaner bag. Then vacuum for an instantly clean-smelling home!

44

Pop up a steamy snack.

Microwave popcorn for a quick snack that will steam the air with its mouth-watering, buttery corn smell.

45

Bake bread.

*F*or bread baking without the bread making, buy frozen yeast rolls or loaves. Let them rise and bake, and instantly your kitchen will smell delicious. Or splurge on a bread oven — it will save your time and knuckles and release the scent of homemade bread.

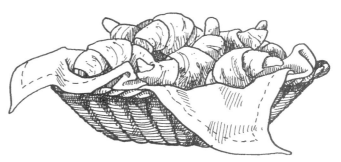

46

Treat with sweets.

Make a cake or batch of brownies before dinner. Place them in the oven when you sit down to eat. The delicious smell of dessert cooking will tempt your nose just when your sweet tooth's ready.

Light a luscious cake candle.

*A*vailable in scents like vanilla, cinnamon spice, and chocolate, yummy-smelling cake candles can be found in many gift and country shops. They last for days and make it smell as if you've baked for hours.

48

Scent a centerpiece.

*F*or a doubly fragrant treat, place a small jar of fragrant flowers in the center of a freshly baked bundt cake. It makes a creative centerpiece and will please all who partake.

Simmer a scent.

Simmer apple cider with cinnamon sticks, cloves, and orange peel for a spicy, fragrant beverage. If you don't have cider on hand, use boiling water. Although you can't drink it, the smell is just as enjoyable. You can also use a small potpourri burner to simmer a liquid fragrance.

50

Freshen up!

*R*emove lingering food aromas with an unscented kitchen candle or room spray. Both will neutralize odors in the air.

51

Refresh your refrigerator.

*W*ipe out your refrigerator and freezer
with a mild fragrant soap and warm water
before going on a big grocery shopping spree.
Discard spoiled items. Restocking your clean,
sweet-smelling refrigera-
tor will be a joy! A box of
baking soda will keep
foods from absorbing
other odors.

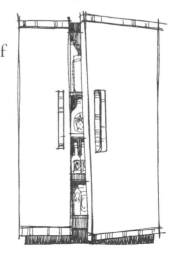

52

Fragrance with fruit.

*F*ill a bowl with the zingy zest of citrus fruit
or soothing scent of apples. When a piece of
citrus fruit looks "tired," cut it in half and grind
it in your garbage disposal to replace unpleasant food odors with a lively, fresh scent.

53

Perfume your pantry.

*S*tore a fruit-scented sachet envelope like apple, peach, or strawberry on a shelf in your kitchen pantry.

54

Breathe easy.

To make the smell of your trash cans, hampers, and diaper pails more tolerable, lay a sachet envelope beneath the plastic lining. You can also use scented plastic liners, scented disks that hang or stick, a sprinkle of baking powder, or an occasional squirt of scented spray.

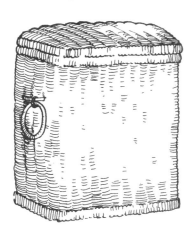

Buy a bouquet.

Select a bunch of sweet-smelling flowers for their scent, as well as their beauty. Scatter the flowers to spread their fragrance throughout your home. Place some in a pretty pitcher or teapot by the kitchen sink.
Breathe in their friendly
fragrance as you
cook and clean up.

56

Cluster casually.

*F*ill a simple mason jar with a casual cluster of sweet-smelling daffodils. Tie a raffia bow around the jar's opening for a finishing touch. Share the joy of fragrance by taking a jar to a friend.

Place a pot in a sunny spot.

$\mathcal{S}$et a pot of fragrant flowers like paperwhites by a sunny window. They will impart a lovely fragrance and last longer than freshly cut flowers.

58

Enjoy the essence of herbs.

Enhance your kitchen with the healthy aroma of fragrant, fresh herbs like rosemary, basil, or lemon thyme. Decorate your kitchen with the delightful scent of an herb wreath, topiary, or bouquet displayed in a pitcher or hung from a pantry door.

Float your fragrance.

Create a scented centerpiece by filling a clear glass bowl with scented floating candles. Toss in a few rose petals to float. Surround the bowl with fresh flowers and greens. Enjoy the fragrant glimmer of the glowing candles.

60

Give guests their own glitter.

$\mathcal{U}$se pretty, stemmed glassware or votive candle holders to hold small scented candles. Light one in front of each place setting. For a

casual touch, use miniature terra cotta pots to hold scented votive candles. Spray paint the pots for color.

Perfume each place setting.

*P*erfume each place setting with a single scent-filled blossom or a petite bouquet of a few fragrant flowers. For a refreshing scent of interesting greenery, add fresh sprigs of mint. Collect and mix and match small, interesting vases or bottles. Just as each guest is unique, let each vase be.

62

Be twice blessed.

Light a scented candle near fresh, sweet-smelling flowers. The fragrant flame will complement the flowers' scent and fill the air with perfume.

Remember with a rose.

For a scented delight at a special dinner, lay a long stem rose in front of each place setting. Tie a fabric ribbon with a handwritten name card to each stem. Give guests their roses as a fragrant memory of the meal.

64

Make a tussie-mussie.

*T*hread a cluster of fragrant flowers and fresh greens through the center of a small paper doily. Twist the underside of the doily around the stems and wrap with floral tape. Use them to enhance place settings or garnish desserts.

Fold in fragrance.

When setting your table, spray the underside of cloth napkins with a light mist of fragrance. For a scented napkin ring, tie a small fabric sachet with ribbon to each cloth napkin. Both touches give a fragrant surprise to friends and family when unfolding their napkins.

66

Create a
sweet-smelling seat.

*T*ie a delightfully scented sachet to each

dining chair with a decorative tassel

or ribbon.

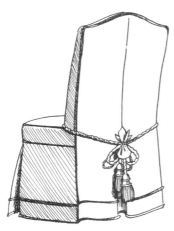

Grow a gardenia.

*L*et the sweet smell of gardenia blossoms enhance your home. Or scent a sunny spot in your home with a dwarf lemon or orange citrus tree. Their broad evergreen leaves produce fragrant white flowers along with small citrus-scented fruits.

68

Fragrance fabrics.

$\mathcal{U}$se a fragranced spray starch when ironing or lightly spritz a favorite cologne right onto your ironing board. The heat of the iron will permeate your fabric with fragrance.

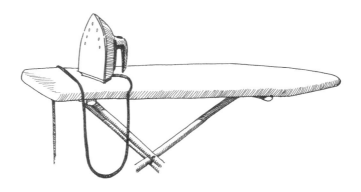

Sleep tight.

$\mathcal{S}$lip a fragrant sachet envelope of vanilla, chamomile, lavender, or rose inside your bed pillow or decorative sham. Drink in the delightful aroma as you drift off to sleep.

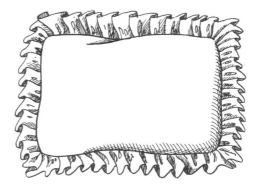

70

Fragrance linens lightly.

Change your bedsheets as often as possible and launder them, as well as your clothes, with a pleasing, perfumed detergent. For a fresh fragrance in between launderings, lift your bedsheets and air them out. Spray them lightly with perfume.

Sprinkle your sheets.

On a warm summer night, before turning in, turn down your sheets and sprinkle them with a fragrant body talc. The perfumed powder will absorb moisture, delighting your nose while keeping your body dry.

72

Store linens with lavender.

When storing table linens, bed linens, and towels, tuck a soothing sachet or a few sprigs of lavender in between them. Lavender is a lovely natural way to fragrance your linens while repelling moths and other pests.

Perfume a pillow.

Spray a pretty throw pillow lightly with pleasant perfume or pin a decorative fabric sachet to it. Toss it in a spot where the scent can be enjoyed.

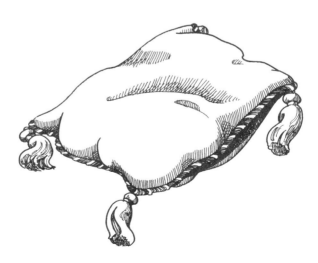

74

Suspend a scent.

*H*ang a bouquet of colorful fresh or dried flowers from a poster bed or ceiling beam. Hang decorative sachets from doorknobs or furniture hardware.

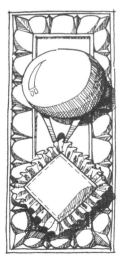

Enjoy a bedside blossom.

A simple rosebud will enhance the air you breathe while you drift off to sleep and as you wake up. For an easy bedside arrangement, cluster colorful blossoms of delicate, sweetly-scented freesia in a small vase or pitcher.

76

Show off a single stem.

*I*n a bud vase, display a single stem of a pink-and-white stargazer lily. Select a stem that still has several closed buds on it. They will gradually open over several days and slowly release their delicate scent.

Save your spot
with scent.

$\mathcal{U}$se a small sachet envelope as a scented bookmark in your Bible or the latest literature beside your bed. The fragrance will make reading so enjoyable you won't want to put the book down!

78

Fragrance a flicker.

*T*o add scent to an unscented pillar or votive candle, dot a few drops of essential oil beneath the wick before burning. Light it, and enjoy the scent as long as the oil lasts.

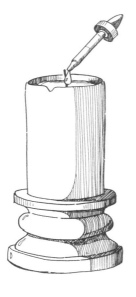

Collect pleasing
perfumes.

*C*ollect a few of your favorite perfumes and display them on a pretty tray on your dresser or vanity. Each day, spray one on that most suits your attitude and attire. For the ultimate luxury, use a lovely, tasseled perfume atomizer to mist on your fragrance.

80

Stick with pins and needles.

*U*se a scented pincushion made of a firm, fabric sachet to display pins and needles. Every time you puncture the pincushion or pull out a pin, the cushion will release its lovely fragrance.

Slip in a sachet.

Slip a sweet-smelling sachet envelope into your clothing drawers. Every time you reach for a garment, your spirits will be lifted. Surprise those you love by hiding scented sachet envelopes in their dresser drawers: men usually prefer spicy scents; young children like fruit scents.

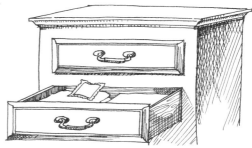

82

Line drawers in luxury.

*F*or a splurge of scent, line your dresser or desk drawers with pretty, perfumed papers. Rubber cement the paper in place. To replenish the fragrance, spray a few squirts of perfume on paper.

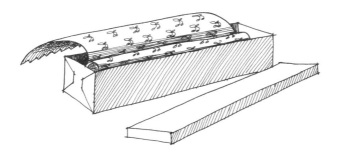

Be my guest.

What's more welcoming than a wonderful fragrance? Greet guests to your home with bedside flowers and a small gift basket filled with perfumed products to scent their bodies.

84

Have sweet-smelling feet.

Use cedar shoe trees or clear plastic boxes with sachets to store your shoes. Both will keep your feet smelling sweet and your shoes in tip-top shape. To absorb bad odors and moisture, occasionally sprinkle shoes with a fragrant powder mixed with baking soda.

Hang it up!

*U*se scented padded hangers to bring pleasant fragrance and shoulder protection to your nicer garments.

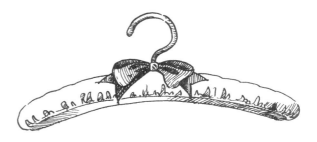

86

Stash a scent.

*L*ike a squirrel stashes nuts to savor for a later time, stow away surprises like scented soaps, lavender bundles, or cedar blocks in your off-season clothing to fragrance and protect it.

Pack a perfume.

Store sachets in unused luggage. Next time you travel, keep the sachet in your suitcase to keep it smelling fresh.

88

Spray away!

*P*lace a can of scented room spray in a visible spot in each bathroom of your home. Celebrate the seasons by changing the scents of your sprays. Gardenia in the spring. Pine in the winter.

Strike a match.

*T*he charcoal smell of a burnt match can instantly override unpleasant odors and neutralize a room's fragrance. If you choose to spray air freshener after lighting a match, a light spray is all you will need.

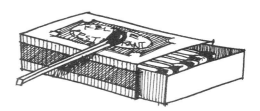

90

Soak in a scent.

When drawing a hot bath, fragrance your bath water with a lovely scent. Give yourself time to soak, savor the smell, and thank God for the many blessings in your life. For a lively, zesty smell, float several rings of thinly sliced lemon in your bathwater.

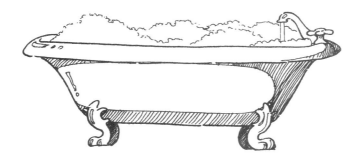

Soothe with scented candles.

*D*im the lights while bathing, and burn a scented candle beside your bathtub. The fragrant flicker will quiet you. Place the candle in a safe spot and let young children enjoy

its soothing scent during their bath time too.

92

Mist in menthol.

*F*or a menthol treat, tie a bouquet or wreath of eucalyptus to your showerhead with a few strands of raffia. Moisture from a steamy, hot shower will release its stimulating scent.

Scent your seashells.

*A*dorn your bathroom shelves with scented seashells. To fragrance, soak small shells in essential oil or dot larger shells with a few drops of oil in their centers.

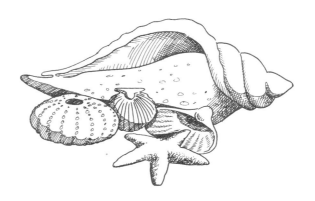

94

Plug it in.

*P*urchase an appealing room freshener that plugs into a standard electrical outlet.

After you plug it in, forget about it! It is safe and easy and will fragrance any room for weeks.

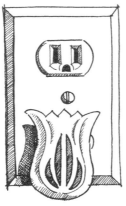

95

Scent a tank.

*F*ragrance and clean your toilet bowl with one of the many products available. Whether they hang on the side of the bowl or drop in the bottom of the tank, all give a whiff of freshness.

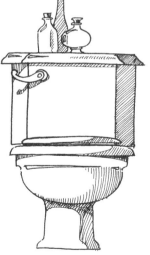

96

Dish up delightful soaps.

*F*ill a pretty dish in your powder room with small scented soaps. Family and friends will enjoy the fragrant treat as they wash their hands. Let children pick their favorite fragrances and shapes for their bath soaps. They will lather up with delight.

Select similar scents.

*W*hen choosing products to clean your home or body, notice the fragrances that please you most. The more products of the same scent you use, the more enticing that fragrance will be.

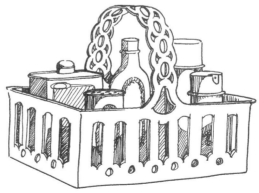

98

Avoid morning breath.

*D*o yourself and those you love a favor by fragrancing your breath with a refreshing mouthwash every morning.

Give it away!

*W*hen wrapping gifts, top them off with a touch of fragrance. Tie a rose, sachet, or cinnamon stick in the bow.

100

Lather in loveliness.

*B*efore crawling into bed at night, clean your body by lathering up with scented soap and rinsing in a quick hot shower or a long warm bath. Top yourself off with a sprinkle of favorite-smelling bath powder.

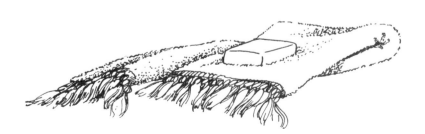

101

Fill your home with his fragrance.

The most satisfying and long-lasting scent in any home is the spiritual fragrance released from a Christ-filled heart. Fill your heart and mind with God's Word and allow the "sweet aroma" of his life to fill your home.

More from Terry Willits . . .

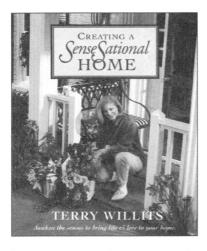

Creating a SenseSational Home is the complete guide to discover how awakening the five senses of sight, smell, taste, touch, and sound can create an atmosphere of love and cheer. From warmly-lit entrances that welcome family and friends to comfortable, homey interiors that invite them to stay and unwind . . . from fragrant bouquets to the tranquil ticking of a clock . . . *Creating a SenseSational Home* shows you simple and affordable ways to turn your home into a relaxing, inviting, and refreshing environment.

ISBN 0-310-20223-X
$19.99

ZondervanPublishingHouse
Grand Rapids, Michigan
http://www.zondervan.com

A Division of HarperCollins*Publishers*

America Online
AOL Keyword:zon